Nanotechnology

by Rebecca L. Johnson

Table of Contents

Get Started	inside front cover
A New Science	2
Stronger and Better	4
Helpers and Healers	5
Tools of the Future	6
Respond and Go Beyond	8
Stretch Your Brain	8
Interpret a Diagram	inside back cover

A New Science

Mmmm! You like lots of grape jelly on your peanut butter sandwich. You take a bite. Oh no! Jelly drips out of the sandwich and lands on your yellow shirt.

Grape jelly usually leaves a purple stain that is very hard to wash out, but this shirt is different. When you wipe the jelly away, there is no stain. The shirt looks just like new. Why?

The shirt remains spotless because the cloth is covered with billions of extremely tiny **particles**. The particles keep the jelly from sticking to the cloth. The particles were created by a new science called **nanotechnology**.

Watch out! He's lucky his shirt is covered in nanoparticles! They will keep the jelly from staining his shirt.

Nanotechnology is the science of putting **atoms** and **molecules** together to make new materials and machines. These new materials and machines are so small that they are invisible to the human eye. They are so small that they are measured in nanometers.

The invisible particles on fabric that keep jelly from sticking are just a few nanometers across. How tiny is a nanometer? A nanometer is one-billionth of a meter. A nanoparticle is about one million times smaller than a particle of sand!

I DIDN'T KNOW THAT!

The *nano* in nanotechnology comes from the Greek word, *nanos*. It means "dwarf." A Japanese scientist, Dr. Norio Taniguchi, first used the word *nanotechnology* in 1974.

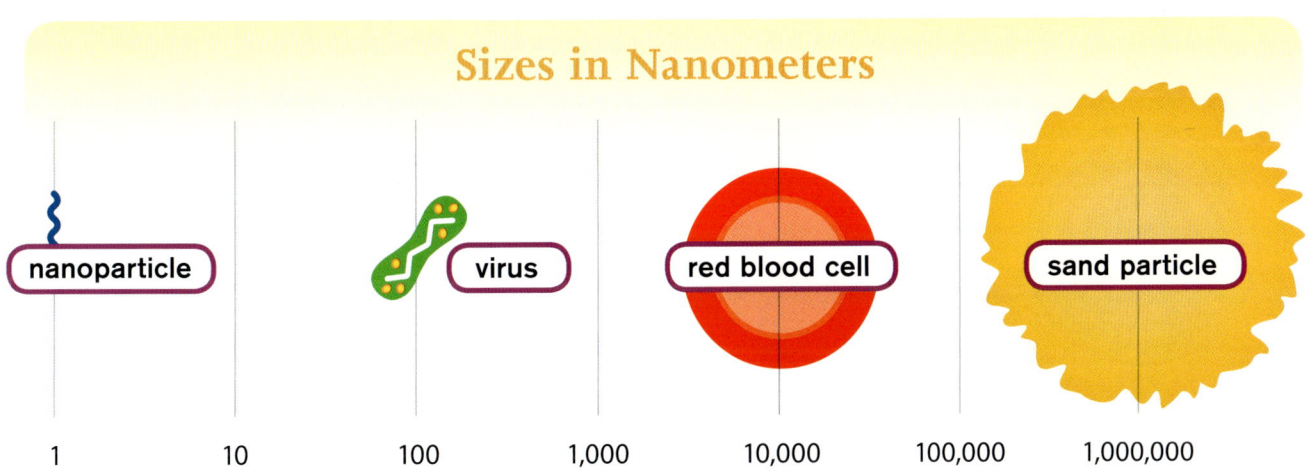

Sizes in Nanometers

| nanoparticle | virus | red blood cell | sand particle |

1   10   100   1,000   10,000   100,000   1,000,000

Super small! How many nanoparticles would you need to stretch across a red blood cell?

Connect Skills to Language

Use the text, pictures, and what you already know to **draw conclusions** about nanotechnology. What kinds of businesses might be interested in clothing that has nanoparticles? How could this clothing be useful to them?

You can use sentences like these as you draw conclusions to answer the questions:

From the text and pictures, I learned that _____.

I already know that _____.

Therefore, I think that _____.

Stronger and Better

Scientists have developed different kinds of nanoparticles. Each kind of nanoparticle has its own special **properties**. A nanoparticle might be light, strong, sticky, or not sticky. Different nanoparticles have different properties.

Scientists are using nanoparticles to make many everyday objects better. The properties of other kinds of matter, such as glass, can be changed by adding nanoparticles. When glass is coated with nanoparticles, water doesn't stick to it. Nanoparticles are also being used to lock air inside tennis balls. The balls don't lose air, so they don't lose their bounce.

Invisible! Nanoparticles cover the inside of this tennis ball to prevent air from escaping.

without nanoparticles

with nanoparticles

Always clear! When scientists coat window glass with nanoparticles, rainwater slides right off.

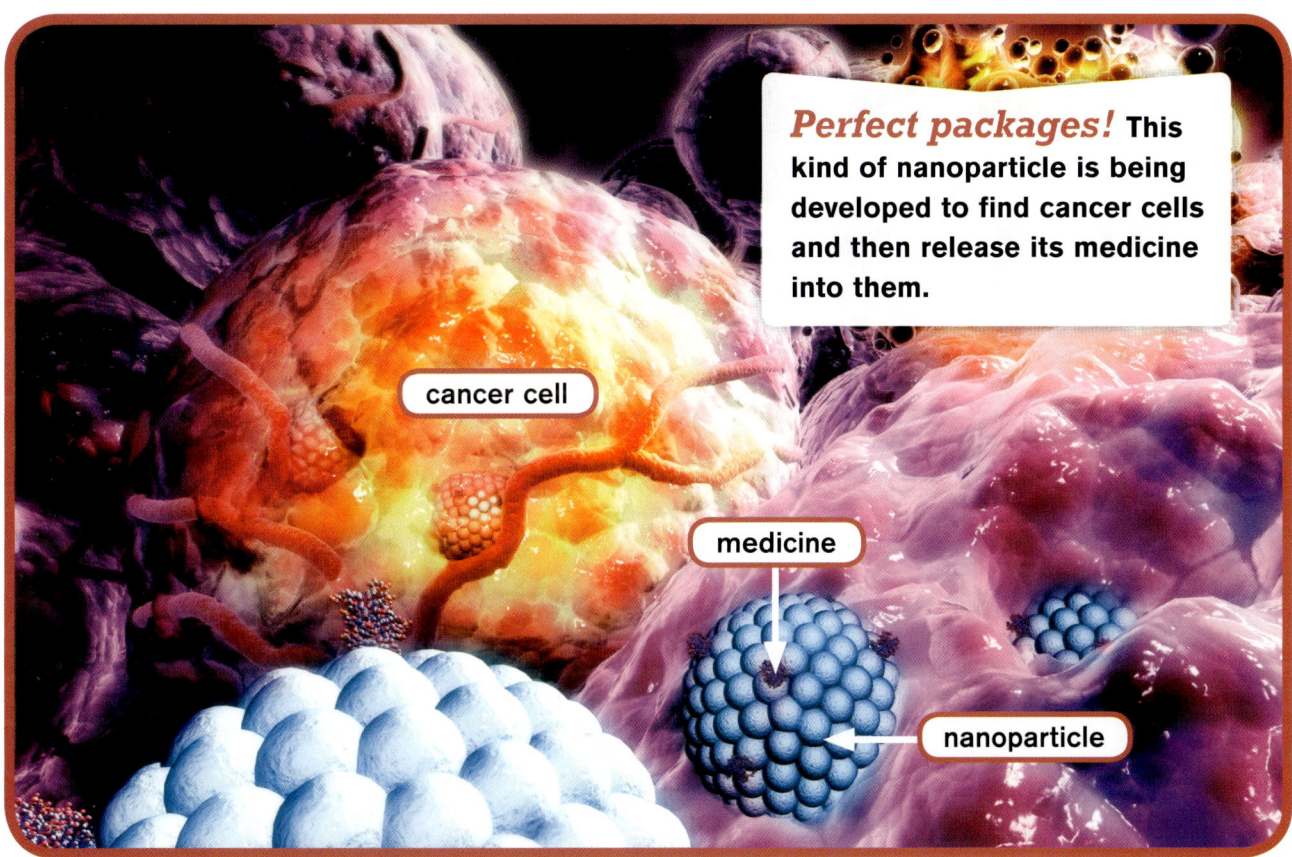

Perfect packages! This kind of nanoparticle is being developed to find cancer cells and then release its medicine into them.

cancer cell

medicine

nanoparticle

Helpers and Healers

Some new bandages contain nanoparticles that destroy germs. When a person covers a cut with a bandage, the nanoparticles begin working. Thanks to the nanoparticles, cuts heal faster.

Nanoparticles may soon help fight diseases like cancer. Scientists are developing nanoparticles that can locate cancer cells. When the particles find cancer cells, the particles stick to them. Cancer cells covered with nanoparticles are easier for doctors to find and destroy.

Other scientists are developing ball-shaped nanoparticles with space inside to contain medicine. These nanoparticles would deliver medicine directly to the inside of cells.

Connect Skills to Strategies

Why is nanotechnology especially useful inside the human body? To answer this question, **draw a conclusion**. Use clues in the text and photos. You can also use what you already know.

Now ask and answer your own questions about nanotechnology and nanoparticles. Then explain how **asking questions** as you read can help you **draw conclusions**.

Tools of the Future

Scientists are also putting nanoparticles together to make the world's smallest machines. They call them "nanomachines."

So far, scientists have made only very simple nanomachines. But scientists are working to create more **complex** types called **nanobots**. Nanobots are super-small robots.

For example, some nanobots might work inside a computer. They could constantly repair parts. Nanobots could also work inside people, repairing damaged body parts or even building new ones!

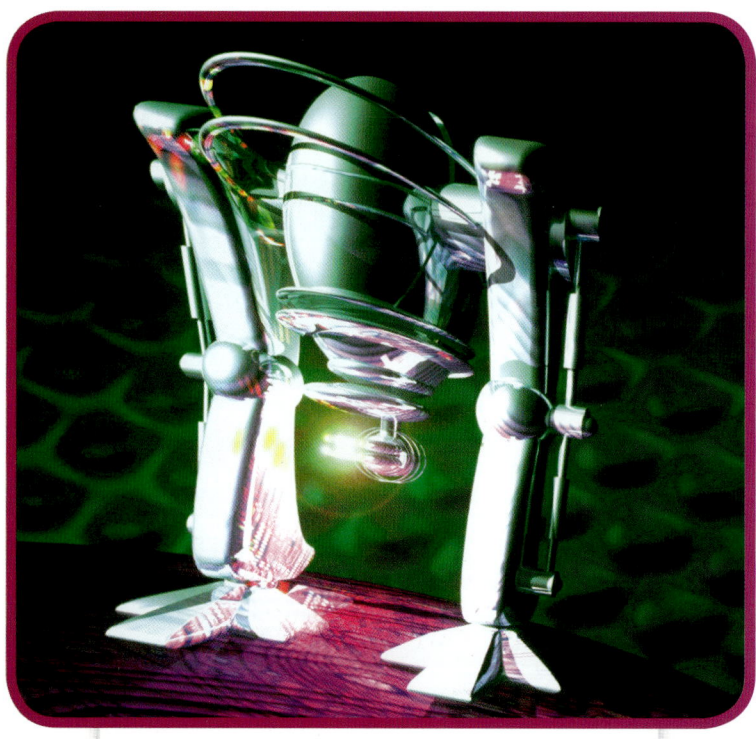

Tech support! Someday a nanobot like this might be able to fix your computer before it crashes!

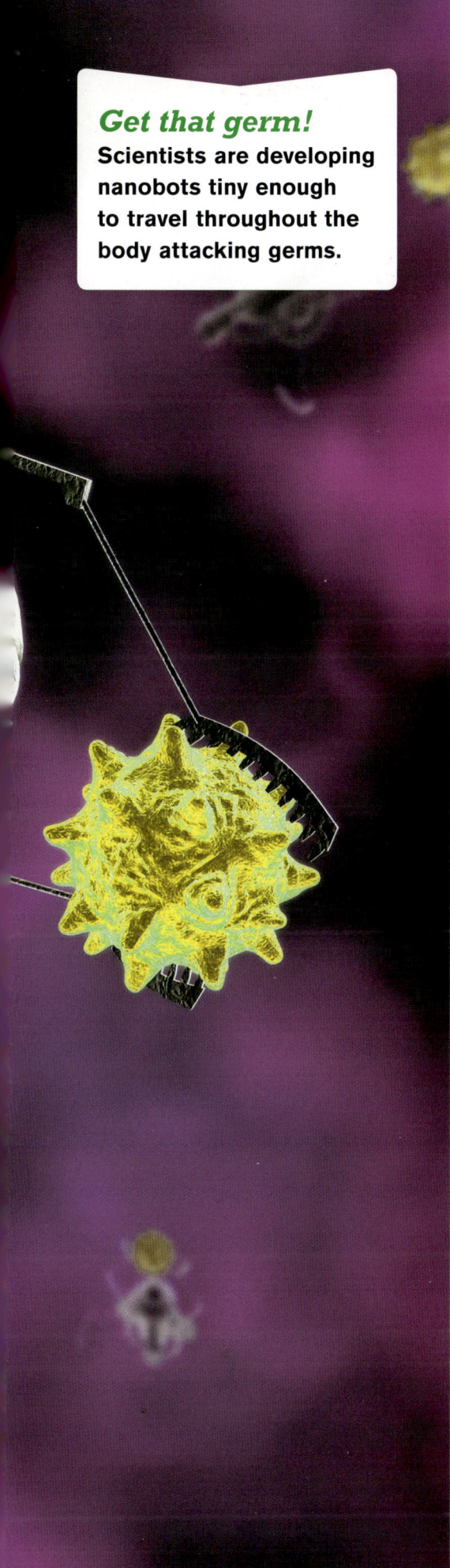

Get that germ!
Scientists are developing nanobots tiny enough to travel throughout the body attacking germs.

Some people worry about nanobots. If scientists do build these tiny nanomachines, people wonder if they will be safe. For example, what would happen if these nanobots broke down and started doing their jobs incorrectly?

No one really knows how nanobots might behave in the future. Nanotechnology will probably make life easier and better in many ways. But there are risks. So scientists are moving ahead slowly and cautiously as they explore this new world of the very, very small.

Put It All Together
Nanotechnology is the science of combining atoms and molecules to create new, extremely tiny things. Some of these new things are materials with special properties. Others are tiny machines that do specific jobs. Nanotechnology may change everyone's life in a big way.

Connect Skills to Your Life
Tell how drawing conclusions can help you:

- figure out how nanotechnology works.
- read and understand other articles about scientific inventions.
- understand how nanotechnology might affect your own life.

Respond and Go Beyond

Share Ideas — After Reading

What is nanotechnology?
Share what you learned with a partner.

Connect Skills to *Nanotechnology*

Use a Chart to Draw Conclusions

Create a flow chart like this one. Ask a question about nanotechnology. Draw a conclusion to answer the question. Share your conclusion with a partner.

Use the Strategy Do you usually ask questions as you read? Go back, reread the text, and think of questions for the chart.

My Question: How can nanotechnology help make housework easier?	→	What The Text Says:
My Conclusion:	←	What I Already Know:

Write About It!

It is now 50 years in the future. Write a news article for that year.
- Describe a nanotechnology that is common.
- Draw conclusions about how nanotechnology has changed.

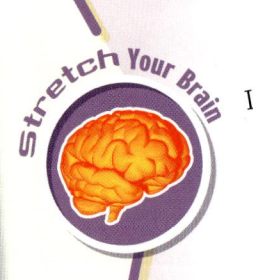
Stretch Your Brain

Create a Nanobot!

Imagine you are a nanotechnology expert. Design a new nanobot. Draw a picture of it and write a description of its special job.

8